Loco-Ha
Passenger Trains
Since the 1980s

ANDY FLOWERS

BRITAIN'S RAILWAYS SERIES, VOLUME 1

Front cover image: On Friday 21 June 2018, Class 33 33029, with 57316 trailing on the rear, passes Burneside on 2Z05, the 12:40 Oxenholme to Windermere. It was the first ever visit by a Class 33 to the branch. The trains were well filled with bashers for these trips, with subsidy and logistics meaning that no fares were taken on the services. Earlier in the week, 37669 had also appeared and the following week a Class 47 was used.

Title page image: 43317 arrived at Edinburgh on a service from London King's Cross on 17 October 2019. December 2019 saw the end of the use of HSTs on LNER services on the East Coast Main Line, following the introduction of bi-mode Azuma units.

Contents page image: 68027 at York on 14 November 2019 on 1E51, the 19:56 Liverpool Lime Street–Scarborough. The Class 68s are still being introduced to TPE services, with many delays due to staff training issues and stock teething problems. The TPE Class 68s may prove to be the last booked diesel locomotives on timetabled services over the East Coast Main Line and the UK rail network as a whole.

Glossary

Bagpipe – A Class 33/1 (fitted with waist-level piping for working with Southern Region EMUs).

Basher – A locomotive haulage fan.

DVT – Driving Van Trailer.

ECS – Empty Coaching Stock.

ETH – Electric Train Heating.

Flirt unit – Fast Light Intercity and Regional Train, a type of multiple-unit train made by Stadler of Switzerland.

Full circle – The whole trip around the Fife Circle (Edinburgh Commuter Trains).

Hoover – A Class 50 (so named because of one of its distinctive sounds).

LUL – London Underground Limited.

The Mule – The line from Waterloo to Exeter (a good way to accumulate mileage).

Nova 3 – The marketing name for TransPennine Express Class 68 hauled services (Nova 1 and Nova 2 are multiple units).

Pauper's Wag – The Wag without on-train dining (see below).

Peaks – Class 44s, 45s and 46s. They were so named as the Class 44s were named after famous mountains and all 3 classes are similar.

Slim Jim – A Class 33 with a narrow bodyshell that could be used on lines with narrow tunnels.

Wag – Prestige service sponsored by the Welsh Assembly Government.

Wherry Lines – The branch lines from Norwich to Great Yarmouth and Lowestoft.

Published by Key Books
An imprint of Key Publishing Ltd
PO Box 100
Stamford
Lincs PE19 1XQ

www.keypublishing.com

The right of Andy Flowers to be identified as the author of this book has been asserted in accordance with the Copyright, Designs and Patents Act 1988 Sections 77 and 78.

ISBN 978 1 913295 72 1

20 21 22 23 24 10 9 8 7 6 5 4 3 2 1

Typeset by Aura Technology and Software Services, India.

Contents

Introduction

To the average member of the public all railway enthusiasts are branded as 'trainspotters', with all the connotations that come with the term. In reality, there are many different types of rail enthusiast, including genuine trainspotters who write down the numbers of locomotives, multiple units, coaches and even wagons, with the aim of viewing them all. Some enthusiasts are photographers, travelling often to out-of-the-way lineside locations to capture shots of rare, or sometimes commonplace, trains, for posterity.

From around 1980 onwards, one of the most common, and popular, forms of railway enthusiasm was 'bashing' – essentially travelling on train services, generally locomotive hauled, with the aim of either being hauled by as many locomotives as possible (preferably each example of each class), or accumulating mileage (or travel) over rare track (track not usually used for passenger services) with their particular class of locomotive. Freight locomotives appearing on passenger trains were particularly sought after, often being a new loco for haulage or 'line in the book'. Other 'bashers' include track bashers, those who attempt to travel on as many stretches of line as possible, particularly rare freight lines, often colouring in the definitive Quail Atlas to record their travels.

Earlier incarnations of the term bashing included 'gricing' and 'gricers' and more latterly, 'cranks' and 'cranking' – though this later term often, nowadays, also encompasses anyone who is in any way interested in railways, or 'cranky', as opposed to non-enthusiast 'normals'.

Some classes of locomotive proved very popular with haulage enthusiasts, possibly starting with the Class 52 'Westerns' on the Western Region, Class 55 'Deltics' on the Eastern Region and Class 40s over much of the network north of the Thames. In later years, other classes, such as the 37s, 45s, 46s and 50s, attracted their own dedicated followings and near the end of locomotive haulage on many routes the ubiquitous Class 47s also developed a group of dedicated fans.

The last 40 years has seen a gradual decline in the extent and variety of locomotive-hauled services on Britain's railways, and more recent years have seen the increased popularity of heritage lines, or foreign travel, as a result. Despite this, some recent developments – including the Class 68s on Chiltern, and now TransPennine Express, services – have seen a slight upsurge in the bashing hobby and this will hopefully continue for a few years to come.

This book details the varied services and locomotives enjoyed by bashers, such as I, over the last 40 years. Some of the earlier photographs were taken on Praktica and Zenith cameras, older 35mm film designs from manufacturers based behind the Iron Curtain. While results were not always top-notch, and have been made even worse in some cases here by scanning, the cameras themselves proved cheap and reliable. Quality has improved over the years as technology has advanced and I've been able to afford better equipment. Hopefully, the earlier shots shown here will still be of acceptable quality to most readers.

Future books will focus on individual classes, lines and/or eras. I hope that the photos contained herein evoke many happy memories for readers and I look forward to presenting more examples, and tales from the archives.

Chapter 1

The 1980s

For many bashers, the 1980s was the Golden Age of locomotive haulage on British Rail, with many locomotive-hauled services and a variety of first-generation diesel locomotives still in service over most of the national rail network. Ticket prices, including rovers, were still good value and the large number of fellow enthusiasts also participating in the hobby ensured a vibrant social scene, with many interesting characters.

Class 20s began to appear on a greater number of passenger trains, to unheard of locations including Derby, Crewe, Llandudno and Blackpool. 25s, 26s and 27s were still in use, undertaking many of their traditional duties in Scotland and (for the 25s) running Crewe–Cardiff services, before gradually being displaced by more powerful types towards the end of the decade.

Class 31s started to appear on a large range of regional CrossCountry services with many more converted to provide electric train heating to meet demands for the reliable Type 2s.

On the Southern Region, the Class 33s began to spread their wings, replaced on their traditional Exeter duties by Class 50s but taking over from Class 37s in West Wales, from Class 25s on Crewe–Cardiffs and even appearing in Manchester and on the North Wales Coast.

Class 37s lost some of their traditional duties in East Anglia but gained dutiful employment in Scotland, taking over from Class 37s on the West Highland Line and Class 26s on the Kyle and Far North routes out of Inverness and gaining many fans on these services.

For the Class 40s, the early 1980s saw the type gradually phased out. Initially still appearing in Scotland, on Glasgow–Aberdeen and Inverness trains, and overnight East Coast services, their passenger duties began to contract to the core North Wales Coast route before their final withdrawal in 1985.

Class 45s and 46s lost their key duties on northeast–southwest services to HSTs in the early 1980s. The introduction of HSTs on the Midland Main Line saw the 45/1s displaced onto CrossCountry trains and TransPennine services.

Class 50s took over Waterloo–Exeter services (see above) but were gradually replaced by HSTs on many key Western Region services during the 1980s, being relegated to less prestigious duties such as Paddington to Oxford commuters.

The Deltics only featured in the first two years of the decade, but they went out with a bang, appearing on many railtours and on hitherto untouched services and locations including Liverpool.

Type 5 freight diesels of Classes 56 and 58 became highly prized on railtours, and also appeared occasionally on emergency and planned dragging of electric locomotives (particularly Birmingham to Nuneaton) and also impromptu rescues.

Class 73s began to be used on more passenger services in addition to their nocturnal newspaper traffic. Two pairs even ventured north of Reading on CrossCountry trains.

The Class 81–85s were mostly withdrawn in the 1980s, with only a small number of the 85s still in active service by the end of the decade. The more recently introduced Class 87s, and later, Class 90s, helped to replace the older types, attracting a cult following despite this.

By the end of the decade the introduction of newer DMU types, like the sprinters, had started to greatly reduce the number and variety of locomotive-hauled services, and many bashers began to explore other avenues, like European railways, or even took up other hobbies.

In October 1980, 40106, a celebrity loco (due to it being the only one of its class to retain its original green livery) that was much in demand for railtour duties, waits at Birmingham New Street with the Sundays-only 09:30 Birmingham–Blackpool North. On this day the train headed north via Cannock Chase and the 40 was replaced at Crewe with a Class 86, with a Class 47 taking the train the last few miles into Blackpool.

37180 stands at London King's Cross on Saturday 22 October on an 08:27 relief service from Leeds. The 37 had arrived into Leeds on the Fridays-only service from Bristol and after some shuffling of resources was allocated on the additional to London. After a storming run, exceeding 100mph in several locations, the loco worked back north on an additional 14:03 to Newcastle and terminated at Peterborough due to hot boxes on the 90mph-limited Mark 1 stock.

In January 1981, 40084 pauses at York, steam heating its rake of Mark 1s on a service from Liverpool to Newcastle, ready for a high-speed run northwards, next stop Darlington. Today, Class 68s work trains from Liverpool into the same platform and, in contrast to other stations along that route like Manchester and Leeds, the station environment within the listed structure looks very similar.

33012 arrives into Warminster on a Cardiff–Bristol–Warminster service in the summer of 1987. The Class 33s had taken over from Class 31s on these services and provided solid reliable service until their replacement by Sprinter DMUs at the end of the 1980s.

On 14 April 1982, 40092 waits at Bangor with 'the Bangor', a popular series of return trains between Manchester Victoria and the North Wales resort that for many years was a solid Class 40 turn. Unseasonably warm weather on this particular day saw Longsight Depot turn out a rare non-boilered example for the train. This view is no longer possible as the embankment is now totally overgrown.

In the late 1980s, Hereford saw a number of loco-hauled services, including Class 33s on the Crewe–Cardiff trains and Class 47s and Class 50s on the Paddingtons. Here, two Class 33s are crossing on Crewe–Cardiffs, 50036 has arrived from Paddington and a three-car Class 120 'Swindon' DMU is waiting for a platform.

On a summer Sunday in 1986, 50036 runs into Hereford ready to form a train to London Paddington. Class 50s worked some of the Paddington to Hereford services over the Malvern Line (via Worcester and Oxford) until the introduction of, initially, Class 47/4s then later HSTs on these trains in the early 1990s. The HSTs themselves have now been withdrawn from the route, their last day on the line being Saturday 18 May 2019.

From the late 1970s, the introduction of HSTs on the East Coast Main Line saw the Class 55 'Deltics' demoted to secondary duties, including, from 1979 onwards, York–Liverpool 'Pennine' services. The first working was 55015 on 1M73, the 11:28 Newcastle–Liverpool Lime Street on 19 June 1979. The author distinctly remembers viewing this passing Ravensthorpe, an unlikely sight, with disbelief! A favourite diagram was 1M62, the 08:49 York–Liverpool and 1E99, the 13:05 return. On a snowy 23 December 1981, 55009 waits at Dewsbury on the 13:05 Liverpool Lime Street–York.

By the 1980s, Class 40s had been retired from most passenger services, though the North Wales Coast Line, from Chester to Holyhead (with a branch off to Llandudno), proved a happy hunting ground for the type. On a summer Saturday many examples of the class could be found on the seasonal additional services operated by BR for holidaymakers. One particular solid turn was the 07:53 Leeds–Llandudno, here waiting at the junction for another 40 to pass on a Euston service.

On 14 April 1982, 40092 is ready to depart back to Manchester on 'the Bangor'. Looking at this bodyside view, the absence of boiler water tanks can be seen clearly, together with a bodyside scar – a feature common to many London Midland region 40s – most likely from negotiating a tight curve near Guide bridge.

40024 at Leeds on 21 December 1981 on a Manchester Victoria–Newcastle relief. The Christmas period often saw BR run a number of additional workings over the main Pennine route via Diggle, often using steam heat only Mark 1 stock, giving haulage enthusiasts prime opportunities to experience Class 40s on steam-heated passenger services over the Christmas period.

On 5 September 1981, 40106 stands ready with the 08:16 Bradford Exchange–Blackpool North via Copy Pit – the last booked Class 40 on a service train over Copy Pit. In the background, a Class 03 shunter is seen with the portion of a train from King's Cross.

The Class 81-85 25kV AC electric locos, known by enthusiasts as 'roarers' due to their distinctive loud fan sound, were popular with haulage fans, being generally rarer on passenger workings than the more powerful Class 86s and 87s. Inter-regional workings, such as this Manchester service, were common passenger duties. 85040 can be seen here at Stockport on 23 December 1981.

BR ran a series of additional services from Blythe Bridge to Blackpool and Llandudno for holidaymakers. The stock and locos were supplied from Derby Etches Park with Toton allocated 20s as the motive power. 20218 and 20099 stand at Blackpool North on 1T09, the 18:42 to Blythe Bridge on 6 July 1989, ready to transport hundreds of drenched holidaymakers back to the Potteries.

45105 passes Heaton Lodge East Junction on a Liverpool to York TransPennine service in the mid-1980s.

On 27 December 1981, 55009 *Alycidon* gets ready to leave Liverpool Lime Street on the 19:10 to York, complete with 'Trans-Pennine Deltic Lament' headboard. The loco had arrived on the 12:05 Newcastle–Liverpool, taking the train over at York. This was advertised by BR as the last Deltic out of Liverpool, though 55002 worked a few days later, and other members of the class have appeared on railtours there in the preservation era.

On 26 September 1989, 20199 and 20202 stand at Derby after working 2P82, the 17:27 Llandudno–Derby. These services proved to be popular with enthusiasts and holidaymakers alike, the usual rolling stock on this route being all stations two-coach Sprinter DMUs, which were slow and cramped with little luggage space.

On 10 February 1982, Class 25 25034 (standing in for an unavailable Class 31) waits at Nuneaton on the 18:15 Birmingham New Street to Norwich service. This was a popular train with haulage enthusiasts, apart from occasionally being allocated a Class 25 (which usually worked the train as far as Peterborough only) it also stopped at Water Orton for the benefit of those on West Midlands travelcards (and also normal commuters).

In early 1982 Class 31/4 31407 stands at Dewsbury on a Liverpool Lime Street–York service after a fresh fall of snow, the low sun direct into the camera severely testing the optics of the Russian-built Zenit camera. Class 31s were very uncommon on TransPennine services until later in the 1980s - Deltics and Class 40s being the more usual substitute motive power for unavailable Class 45s or 47s.

Working its last ever passenger service for BR Deltic, 55002 *The King's Own Yorkshire Light Infantry* leaves Dewsbury on 1E98, the 12:05 Liverpool Lime Street–York, on 30 December 1981. This was a few days after the advertised final TransPennine working, 55002 being turned out on test for the final tour on the Saturday. After being declared a failure at York it entered the Great Hall at the National Railway Museum.

In a scene that is almost unrecognisable today, 40162 (the last Class 40 with operable Headcode Display Blinds) has arrived at Manchester Victoria on 21 August 1982 on 1J53, the 15:17 from Holyhead. Redevelopment of the whole station, including an overall roof has transformed this view.

Near the end of their careers, the Deltics became popular for railtour duties. On 29 December 1981, 55009 stands at Leeds, steaming a rake of Mark 1s forming the 'Deltic Executive'. Leeds station, now expanded and electrified, is virtually indistinguishable today from this view almost 40 years ago.

After arriving from Nuneaton the previous evening, 56004 leads an additional, diverted, 07:10 to Manchester Piccadilly BR InterCity West Coast service out of Barlow's Train Shed (Saint Pancras) on 21 July 1989.

Early in 1985, an unidentified Class 85 arrives at Coventry on a London Euston to Birmingham New Street service. Of interest is the mix of rolling stock – Mark 1s and air-conditioned and pressure-ventilated Mark 2s, all in the same rake of coaching stock.

56104 with 47503 on 1E11, the 12:42 Carlisle–Leeds on Saturday 4 November 1989. British Rail Regional Railways experimented with providing rare freight locos on top of the usual Class 47s to boost passenger numbers during the month. The move was very successful, with up to 796 passengers on some services.

Class 33/1 33112 *Templecombe* stands at Weymouth on a service from London Waterloo in early 1988. Electrification of the line through to the Dorset resort ended the need for 33/1 haulage to and from Bournemouth. The new third-rail DC electrification equipment can be seen in the foreground.

Class 50 50050 arrives at Banbury in 1989. Class 50s had a long association with trains on the London Paddington to Birmingham corridor (via Solihull and/or Coventry). Workings included dedicated London–Birmingham/ Wolverhampton trains and also a number of inter-regional services, including the quirky morning London Paddington–Hull (which was a Class 50 as far as Birmingham New Street).

In 1988, 50043 stands at Exeter Saint Davids after arrival on a service from London Waterloo via 'the Mule'.

In Winter 1989, 50026 waits at Oxford with a commuter service to London Paddington. The Mark 2 coaches provided for this BR Network South East service are a world apart in terms of comfort from the airline-style seating provided in the DMUs used by current operators.

In 1989, unique thyristor-controlled Class 87/1 87101 *Stephenson* arrives at London Euston on a service from Birmingham New Street. In the adjoining platform stands a relatively brand-new Class 90 on a service from Manchester Piccadilly.

In the summer of 1989, an unidentified Class 86/4 arrives at Coventry on a Birmingham New Street–London Euston service. Of note, is the use of a BR Mark 1 BG as the brake on these services, in a time before DVTs and the need for shunt release locomotives at termini.

Class 37/4 37426 arrives at Crewe on a Liverpool Lime Street–Cardiff Central service in 1988. After conversion to ETH-capable locos, the Class 37/4s found gainful employment early on with Caledonian Sleeper services to Fort William and trains on the Crewe–Cardiff 'Marches' line.

In the 1980s, 33008 *Eastleigh* was repainted into its original two-tone green British Railways colours. Here, it is seen arriving at Salisbury in early 1987 on a Bristol Temple Meads to Portsmouth Harbour service.

By 1987, Class 33s were becoming less common on London Waterloo–Exeter Saint Davids services, with Class 47s also becoming spare and ready to stand in when no Class 50s were available for services. Here, an unidentified Class 33/0 nears Honiton with an up service.

In February 1989, 37417 waits at Kyle of Lochalsh with the early morning service to Inverness. The Class 37/4's electric train heating was much needed on this particular morning as snow covered the station and the hills on the Isle of Skye in the background.

In 1989, Class 50 50045 stands waiting time at Cheltenham Spa after a rousing 100mph+ run down from Birmingham New Street. By this time, Class 50s were becoming less common on inter-regional workings such as this. The rake of stock is of interest, comprising a Mark 1, several pressure-ventilated earlier Mark 2s and an air-conditioned, later, Mark 2, all with mixed liveries.

20090 and 20107 stand at Llandudno Junction on 26 June 1989, in the sidings. They were due to work 1T07, the 18:10 to Blythe Bridge, later in the day. An unidentified Class 47 stands with a Stoke service, while the ubiquitous bashers' Head bag on the platform gives a very 1980s feel.

47556 passes Heaton Lodge East Junction on a Liverpool–York TransPennine service in the early 1980s. BR built a dive under at this location to enable grade separation due to high traffic levels and conflicting movements at the junction.

Chapter 2

The 1990s

By the 1990s many of the main-line diesels introduced in the 1950s and 1960s had either been withdrawn or were largely restricted to freight duties as BR modernised its passenger fleet with new locomotives and replaced many locomotive-hauled services with new Sprinter and second-generation fresh unit designs.

Popular classes that ended in the 1980s included Class 25s, 40s, 45s, 46s and Deltics, though many examples of these types ended up preserved on heritage railways, with the rise of diesel enthusiasm in the 1970s and 80s translating into a ready supply of fans willing to invest money in restoring their favourite locomotives.

Sectorisation had seen locomotives allocated to different pools, limiting the number of locomotives likely to appear on any given train. Funding cutbacks had seen the closure of some lines and stations and many additional summer Saturday dated services (a welcome source of rare freight locomotive haulage for haulage enthusiasts) had been withdrawn as cost cutting began to bite.

Despite this general mood of gloom there were still many reasons for bashers to venture out on the rail network. While steam heat had all been withdrawn in the 80s the conversion of many additional locomotives of Classes 31, 37 and 47 to provide electric train heating ensured that locomotive haulage would be around for a few years to come.

Class 20s continued to work to Skegness, and occasionally other destinations too. The ever reliable, and increasingly popular, Class 37s began to branch out on new services in Scotland, the North West and the Welsh Marches. Many CrossCountry services became the sole responsibility of Class 47s, bringing a whole new army of fans for this well-travelled class.

Towards the middle and the end of the decade, privatisation brought about some of the biggest changes in the railway in many decades, with freight and passenger operators concentrating their fleets into even smaller subsectors, further reducing the range and variety of available locomotives to be found on passenger services.

One consequence of railway privatisation that couldn't have been foreseen by any commentators was the return of Deltics to main-line timetabled passenger services. 55022, renumbered to its former D9000 branding and repainted into its original two-tone green livery, was hired by Virgin CrossCountry for a number of passenger services, including a regular summer Saturday turn from Birmingham to Ramsgate and return. D9000 made appearances all over the network, ranging from Plymouth, to Bournemouth, Edinburgh, Glasgow and Newcastle. Though the hire in is unlikely to have generated any profits it certainly generated a lot of interest and reawakened the interest of many bashers, many of whom had never had haulage previously with a Deltic on a service train.

In 1999 the 'Train for Life' saw three Class 20s sent to Kosovo with a trainload of medical supplies and logistical equipment. Though the train was not available for bashers the onboard rail staff, consultants and journalists enjoyed perhaps the rarest and most incredible haulage of all time behind any British locomotives.

20215 and 20142 are seen near Worksop on an additional working as part of Worksop Open Day, held on 1 September 1992. Brand new Class 60 60069 *Humphry Davy* provided the motive power at the other end of the stock.

56007 approaches Worksop with an additional working from Doncaster as part of Worksop Open Day, held on 1 September 1992. Class 58 58040 *Cottam Power Station* was the tail-end loco.

In 1998 and 1999, Virgin CrossCountry hired D9000 (55022) to work a summer Saturday-only diagram from Birmingham to Ramsgate and return. The trains involved were 1O99, the 06:58 Birmingham New Street–Ramsgate and 1S87, the 11:26/12:10 Ramsgate to Glasgow – it went out via the West Coast Main Line and Kensington Olympia and worked back as far as Birmingham, via Reading and Oxford on the return.

The ageing and increasingly unreliable Class 47/8 'Twin-Tank' long-range CrossCountry diesels gave ample opportunities in later years for exotic substitutions and rescue locos. One good prospect for a non-47 'kickout' from the Birmingham area was 1O38, the 09:10 Edinburgh–Bournemouth, which was allocated 37198 on 18 July 1998.

The unreliability of the Class 47/8 'Twin-Tank' long-range CrossCountry locos, used by Virgin until the introduction of their Voyager units, led to many impromptu Type 5 diesel loco appearances, often following failures. Here 56032 is seen at Birmingham International on 5 August 1998 on 1S87, the 14:18 London Paddington–Edinburgh Waverley service.

37057 and Mainline Blue-liveried 37371 wait at Birmingham New Street on 4 July 1999 with 1D99, the 23:30 to Holyhead. The lead loco worked the train as far as Chester.

On 30 January 1999, 31427 waits to take a Virgin CrossCountry service from Birmingham International to Preston. A wide variety of locos could be found substituting for Class 47/8s on CrossCountry services around this time, but the use of a Class 31 was unusual and the Type 2 loco had to work hard to try to keep time on this service, which was timed for a Type 4, a task it valiantly failed to do.

On 22 June 1991, 20019 and 20094 stand at Sheffield after working the 10:38 from Skegness. The first part of the diagram was an 06:30 Sheffield–Skegness. The diagram was booked for a pair of Trainload Coal Class 20s, on hire to Regional Railways, and was a solid turn for the Toton-based freight locos. Here, the 20s wait to take the train ECS back to Derby Etches Park.

Possibly the most unusual and audacious working for any British locomotives was the 'Train for Life' run from Derby to Kosovo in September 1999, following the end of the Kosovo War. The trainload of medical supplies and civil engineering equipment included three DRS Class 20s, 20901, 20902 and 20903, which worked the train over several unelectrified sections on the continent. Here, the Class 20s are fired up in the yard at Decin (just over the border in the Czech Republic) after a run down from Dresden. This train was the first, and possibly the last, time that Class 20s have ever visited the Czech Republic.

On 12 August 1998, EWS hire-in Class 37 37057 stands at Birmingham International with 1F74, the 18:47 Birmingham International–Liverpool Lime Street Virgin Trains CrossCountry service, standing in for an unavailable Class 47/8. The loco had worked in from Manchester Piccadilly earlier.

On 2 April 1999, Class 66 66014 made the debut for the type on a timetabled passenger service, a Crewe–Holyhead and return diagram, substituting for an unavailable Class 37/4. Here, 66014 enters Chester on 1K67, the 12:51 Holyhead–Crewe.

On Sunday 20 September 1998, Class 47 47703 passes Berkswell on a CrossCountry service. The Fragonset-owned loco was on hire to Virgin Trains CrossCountry.

Class 37s joined the long list of classes of diesel locomotive to have worked on the North Wales Coast Line, taking over many regional services between 1993 and 2001, with trains from Holyhead, Bangor and Llandudno to Crewe, Manchester, Birmingham (International and New Street) and Cardiff. Here EWS-liveried 37418 arrives at Bangor on a service from Holyhead to Crewe.

National Railway Museum-owned Class 37 37350 (formerly 37119) hauls a 1Z37, 09:08 Solihull–London Marylebone special, on 14 March 1999, shortly after release from the museum.

In the early hours of 3 August 1998, Class 20s 20306 and 20310 stand at Glasgow Central after dragging a service from London Euston. The Class 20s were attached at Carlisle and worked via the Glasgow and South Western route (via Dumfries).

On Sunday 20 September 1998, unique thyristor-controlled Class 87/1 87101 *Stephenson* passes Berkswell (between Birmingham International and Coventry) on a London Euston–Birmingham New Street service. The 87/1, at the time generally restricted to freight duties, was pressed into action for a few weeks on West Midlands–London Euston Virgin Trains services.

In August 1998, BR Civil Engineering 'Dutch'-liveried Class 73 73107 heads past Kensington Olympia with a Channel Tunnel-bound car-carrying train, working as far as Dollands Moor. The Class 73 will have taken over this service in Wembley Yard. In the background, a London Underground Tube service District Line branch train, formed of D-Stock units, departs for Earl's Court.

On Saturday 20 June 1998, 56019 was provided as traction for a Virgin Trains CrossCountry service for 1O38, the 09:10 from Edinburgh to Bournemouth. The Class 56 worked the service between Birmingham New Street and Bournemouth, standing in for an unavailable Class 47/8. The loco returned (as far as Birmingham New Street) with 1M81, the 18:14 Bournemouth to Manchester Piccadilly.

On Sunday 9 August 1998, Cardiff Railways ran a series of advertised 'relief' trains using Class 50 50031. In reality, these services, advertised in advance, were essentially railtours, starting at Rhymney and running up the Valley Lines to Treherbert and Merthyr Tydfil. Here, 50031 is seen waiting at Pontypridd during an afternoon break. For those travelling on the series of extras, a Valleys Day Ranger ticket was £5.40.

Mainline Freight-liveried Class 37 37216 is a welcome surprise for many enthusiasts as it stands at Birmingham International on 20 May 1999 on 1D99, the 21:52 Birmingham International–Holyhead service. 37216 was one of several 'no heat' locos drafted in after the 37/4 pool was temporarily withdrawn in 1999, following an issue with an equalising beam that fell off 37421. The loco and stock worked back with 1G80, the 03:16 Holyhead to Birmingham International. 37216 is today preserved at the Pontypool and Blaenavon Railway.

1D99, the 23:12 Birmingham International–Holyhead service, was always a favourite with enthusiasts, particularly on a Sunday night when heavy loadings of students and travellers heading for the overnight boat to Ireland meant that the load had to be doubled to eight coaches, and a pair of 37/4s would be allocated.

Class 25 D7672 *Tamworth Castle* (previously 25322/25912) at Leeds on 1M09, the 08:25 Leeds–Carlisle on 24 February 1990, with Class 47 47422 tucked inside for electric train heating. 25912 was temporarily taken back into service by BR in 1987 as a training loco at Holbeck and renumbered D7672. It operated a number of railtours before finally being withdrawn in March 1991. The loco is now preserved at Cheddleton on the North Staffordshire Railway.

On 24 February 1990, BR organised a special traction day over the Settle and Carlisle Line. 26007 is seen here at Leeds piloting 47443 on 1M43, the 10:45 Leeds to Carlisle service, after arriving earlier on 1E09, the 06:34 from Carlisle. 26007 survives to this day, preserved at Barrow Hill.

Another view of the 'Train for Life' from 1999, with 20901, 20902 and 20903, waiting at Svitavy, between Prague and Brno. The train was operated as a freight service and was laid over for several hours at a number of locations en route, allowing passenger, and some freight services, to pass.

Class 58s were unusual on passenger workings, and were largely confined to Birmingham New Street–Nuneaton 'drags', or railtours. The appearance of 58017 on a CrossCountry service at Coventry on 22 August 1998 was something of a rarity. It was deputising for an unavailable Class 47 on 1M81, the 18:14 Bournemouth to Manchester Piccadilly (as far as Birmingham New Street).

Class 50s, displaced by the introduction of HSTs on the Western Region, took over Waterloo–Exeter services from Class 33s from May 1980. The route became very popular with 'Hoover' fans, being nicknamed 'the Mule'. Thirteen Class 50s were provided for nine daily diagrams on the bi-hourly services. The Class 50s were withdrawn from service on the route in 1992 and hauled operations on the line finally ended in 1993.

On Wednesday 19 August 1992, 20090 and 20132 sit at Skegness after arriving on the additional 1Z86 09:26 from Derby. This pair of Class 20s were very prevalent on passenger duty that year and proved to be reliable locos and good performers, appearing on a number of services.

33101 at London Waterloo in 1990, with a 4TC (unpowered Southern Region EMU-style trailer set), ready to form a train to Salisbury. The 'Bagpipe' 33/1s were capable of push-pull working with a wide variety of Southern Region third-rail DC EMUs. In the background, a Class 50 waits its next turn after hauling in a service from Exeter Saint Davids.

On 18 July 1997, the shortage of Class 47s meant that Virgin CrossCountry, unusually, provided a Class 31/4-Class 37/0 combination for 1V96, the 09:10 Edinburgh to Reading and 1M79, the 16:47 Reading to Liverpool. This was a favourite turn for freight substitute locos at the time, with the diesels working between Reading and Birmingham. The pair are seen here rounding the curve at Coventry on the return to New Street.

37678 and 37417 wait time at Kensington Olympia on 9 August 1997 with a summer-dated Saturdays-only service from Birmingham New Street to Ramsgate. Class 37/4 37417 was tucked inside to provide electric train supply for air conditioning (which, from memory, didn't actually work). In 1997, Virgin used a variety of guest locos on this service which ran out via the West Coast Main Line and returned via Oxford.

Class 58s were never common on passenger services, and even less so on CrossCountry ones. Here, we see 58017 at Leamington Spa on 1O38, the 09:10 Edinburgh–Bournemouth, on 22 August 1998.

On 18 November 1997, 89001 waits at King's Cross with 1D33, the 07:50 to Bradford Forster Square. After the usual 110mph run up to Bradford, a delay on the return saw the 'Flying Badger' (so named because of its livery) loco reach a speed of 132.5mph near Huntingdon. The distinctive loco was withdrawn from service shortly afterwards and is now preserved at Barrow Hill.

French freight company CFD bought four Class 20s at the end of the 90s and ran two very popular railtours, one in 1998 and one in 1999. On 16 October 1999, 2001 and 2002 (20035 and 20063) stand at Auxerre Saint Gervais with the empty coaching stock after the second tour (an ADL trip to Cercy-la-Tour). Both locos were eventually repatriated to Britain.

37372 stands at Manchester Piccadilly on 5 August 1997, after rescuing a failed Class 47/8 south of Coventry on 1M05, the 06:03 London Paddington–Manchester Piccadilly. The loco returned south on 1V48, the 12:17 to Plymouth, working the train as far as Birmingham New Street.

Before the large-scale introduction of DMUs in the 1990s, many longer-distance BR Regional Railways trains were formed of Class 31/4s and Mark 1 or Mark 2 coaches. In Summer 1990, 31403 calls at Preston on a Barrow-in-Furness to Manchester Victoria working.

On 10 March 1990, Class 20s 20905 and 20906 piloted Class 47 47422 on an out and back working from Carlisle to Leeds. The Hunslet-Barclay Class 20/9s were usually employed top and tail on weedkilling trains all over the BR network and were a huge draw for enthusiasts; the trains could sometimes have over 600 passengers at points in the journey.

D9000 (55022) arrives at Coventry on 1O99, the 06:58 Birmingham New Street–Ramsgate, on a summer Saturday in 1999. The service was diverted into Platform 2, instead of stopping at the more usual platform 1, because of a points failure, making this photo possible.

After arrival from Llandudno, mixed-livery pair 20138 and 20087 (BR Railfreight Red 20138 and BR Corporate Blue 20087) get ready to run round to take the empty coaches back to Etches Park on 13 September 1991.

Chapter 3

The 2000s

The new millennium brought even further cutbacks in the numbers and variety of locomotive-hauled trains. The withdrawal of loco-hauled services on Virgin Trains West Coast (with the introduction of Class 390 Pendolino EMUs and Class 220 and Class 221 Voyager DMUs) saw London Euston reduced to just two loco-hauled departures a day – the Highland and Lowland Caledonian Sleeper services.

On the East Coast Main Line, by contrast, most services remained loco-hauled, with Class 91s (with an occasional Class 90) together with HSTs provided for most trains. The end of the Class 50s saw London Paddington also largely devoid of conventional locomotive-hauled services to the west, though some Class 47s still worked until around 2004, together with one-off GM Class 57 57601. HSTs still reigned supreme on most Western high-speed trains.

Although diesel-hauled services had become less and less commonplace, there were a few surprises, largely brought about by the short-term hire of locos and stock to substitute for a shortage of multiple units. At the forefront of the new 'niche' loco-hauled services were the still popular and reliable Class 37/4s and the new Class 67s, displaced from their original intended duties on high-speed Royal Mail workings. The fleet found work with new passenger operators and as Thunderbird locos on the East Coast Main Line, providing interesting dragging turns including King's Cross to Peterborough via Cambridge, Peterborough to Doncaster via Lincoln and Carlisle diversions via the Tyne Valley.

While compared to previous decades there were very few large-scale loco-hauled passenger operations, the rare and interesting nature of any that remained managed to keep many enthusiasts interested, though the overall numbers of bashers on the railway declined sharply (save for railtours and one-off advertised special workings).

The open access operator, Wrexham and Shropshire, was formed in 2006, operating services from Wrexham, Shrewsbury and intermediate stations to London Marylebone (the only London station available for the company due to objections from other operators). A combination of unavailability of DMUs and the intention to provide a quality service with full catering saw Class 67s hired with Mark 3 coaches, initially from Cargo D, before their own refurbished stock became available. The service was very well received and attracted a new audience of fans for the Class 67s, and a hitherto unexpected return of loco-hauled high-speed trains to the previously run-down Chiltern route between Banbury and London Marylebone.

Another new train starting in 2008 was the 'Premier Service' from Cardiff to Holyhead and return. Using Mark 2s and Class 57/3s, this train was also ostensibly provided as a luxury service with catering, funded by the Welsh Government to provide a link between North and South Wales using four locos hired from Virgin Trains West Coast (57313–57316). The services were termed the 'Wag Expresses' (after the Welsh Assembly). The locos and stock also worked some additional diagrams to Manchester and Llandudno – termed the 'Paupers Wag' due to a lack of full dining.

Other pockets of loco-hauled travel included Norfolk, where standby rakes of stock were still used regularly on the 'Wherry Lines' between Norwich, Yarmouth and Lowestoft, still hauled by Class 47s during this decade, and also the South West where Class 67s, and for a time Class 57/3s, were used on Cardiff–Taunton trains.

Another unlikely new hotspot for loco-hauled trains was Rhymney with Class 50s, and even Class 33s, returned to passenger service and a Class 50 diagrammed through to Fishguard.

On the Cumbrian Coast, the use of locomotives and stock in 2009, to provide a shuttle service between Workington and Maryport, was the precursor to the more widescale use of locos and stock in the decade to come.

Class 45 45112 stands in the yard at Norwich Tore during the ACoRP weekend in September 2005. The loco had been booked to work some additional services to Great Yarmouth but unfortunately, due to failure, remained a static exhibit in the yard, together with a wide range of other locos, including 87019 and 89001.

In the summer of the year 2000, 37415 approaches Llandudno Junction on a Holyhead–Crewe diagram, while a Class 101 DMU runs empty into the station to form a Blaenau Ffestiniog service.

On 3 September 2002, 86231 passes Canley on the 14:15 Birmingham New Street–London Euston. The Class 86/2s featured heavily on Wolverhampton and Birmingham to London Euston services but were replaced by Pendolino EMUs in 2003. 86231 was one of 13 Class 86s in use with Virgin Trains and was later exported for freight use in Bulgaria in April 2016.

On 11 July 2002, GNER-liveried 43113 propels a service from Aberdeen out of Edinburgh Waverley, south towards King's Cross. Many considered the attractive blue GNER livery one of the best ever applied to the HST fleet.

In October 2004, 67029 was painted into its distinctive silver livery, which matched the EWS Company Train with dedicated DVT. It went on to be named *Royal Diamond* on 12 October 2007, commemorating the 60th wedding anniversary of the Queen and Prince Philip. Here, the loco is on hire to Wrexham and Shropshire, working a Wrexham to London Marylebone service on 3 February 2009 and departing Tame Bridge Parkway for the south.

On Saturday 9 May 2009, 55022 (often referred to by its former pre-TOPS number of D9000) is seen from the turrets of Corfe Castle leaving Corfe station while working the 15:10 Swanage to Norden service during the annual Swanage Railway Diesel Gala. The gala on the Swanage Line is regarded by many as one of the highlights of the diesel calendar on Britain's heritage railways.

Class 73109 *Battle of Britain 50th Anniversary* at London Waterloo on 16 April 2005 in Stagecoach livery on a special additional working to Alton, dragging 3rd-rail EMUs 4-CIG 421398 and 4-VEP 423481. The all-day event, with workings to Basingstoke and Alton, commemorated the last day the loco would work in Stagecoach livery

37408 *Loch Rannoch* was used very extensively on North Wales Coast services and is here seen on a Manchester to Holyhead service near Penmaenmawr. The photo was taken from a popular photo spot, a footbridge over the A55, opposite to a now-closed branch of the Little Chef. The loco was withdrawn on 31 December 2007 and cut up shortly afterwards, on 31 January 2008, at EMR Kingsbury.

While strictly no longer a British locomotive, the ex-Woodhead Class 77 electrics still featured on passenger trains during the time period of this book, albeit in the Netherlands and redesignated as Class 1500s by Nederlandse Spoorwagen (Netherlands State Railways), following their purchase in 1969. Here, 1501 is seen at Den Haag on railtour duty on Saturday 16 June 2001.

The Channel Tunnel shuttle locomotives are notoriously difficult to photograph, the operators taking security very seriously indeed. This shot of 9023, on a passenger shuttle heading for Calais in 2002, was taken from an overbridge during preparation of an article on the shuttle operations. Access was granted by Eurotunnel to take this shot only after an extensive safety briefing and the author was accompanied by members of staff at all times.

37408 gained something of a cult following amongst the ardent followers of the class. The reasons for this are lost in time, though factors may include its reliability, extensive use on passenger services and name (*Loch Rannoch*). Here, the loco is seen drifting down the hill into Holyhead on a service from Crewe on 22 February 2000.

57601 was a speculative rebuild loco, ordered by Porterbrook in 2000, with a Class 47 bodyshell and bogies re-engined with a GM power unit. Its success led to follow on orders for Class 57/3s. 57601 was leased to First Great Western between June 2001 and the end of 2002, and was used on daytime hauled services between London Paddington, Plymouth and Penzance. Here, 57601 is seen at Bath on a train from Paddington on 18 March 2002.

In 1984, a small fleet of Class 73s were assigned to the new non-stop Gatwick Express services, a tradition that lasted until 2005. The service was the first part of BR's Intercity sector to be privatised and by this point had acquired a dedicated fleet of Class 73/2s in InterCity livery operating similarly coloured Mark 2 coaches, like 73212, seen here near Horley station on the approach to the airport.

57301 *Scott Tracy* arrives at Bangor on a Holyhead–Manchester service on 4 December 2008. Arriva Trains Wales hired Class 57/3s from Virgin from January 2006 to work some Cardiff–Holyhead and Holyhead–Manchester trains. The 57/3s, some repainted into ATW livery, were replaced on these services by Class 67s from March 2012.

On 17 October 2004, 37422 arrives at Crewe on an additional relief service from Manchester Piccadilly. The Class 37 went on to perform on passenger services for many more years to come, including in East Anglia on Greater Anglia services from Norwich to Great Yarmouth and Lowestoft.

Diesel shunters were never common on passenger duties, though they could be 'bashed' on some stock movements in the 80s, e.g. at Sheffield as the portions of the Leeds and Newcastle to Poole were combined. On heritage railways the operators recognise the attraction of haulage by diesel shunters and regularly diagram them on trains, particularly during galas. Here, at Lydney, Class 14 D9555 (arguably itself a shunter, though designed for main-line trip freights) brings a train from Norden into the southern terminus of the Dean Forest Railway in 2005.

Class 87 87019 leans into the curve at speed as it travels through Rugby on a London Euston to Wolverhampton service in June 2006. The locomotive, reliveried into LNWR Black in 2005 and renamed *ACoRP The Association of Community Rail Partnerships* (from *Sir Winston Churchill*), was withdrawn on 30 November 2006. The loco was exported to Bulgaria in January 2007 and is still in service there.

On 20 February 2007, with the overhead power switched off due to planned engineering works, 67028 gets ready to drag a Class 91 as far as Newark North Gate on a Leeds Service. The Class 67 maintained three figure speeds for much of the journey, arriving 10 minutes early into Newark.

57309 *Brains* is seen at Holyhead in 2007. The Class 57/3 'Bodysnatcher' – named after they were built using the bodyshells of Class 47 donors with GM power units installed – will work the train as far as Crewe, where the Class 390 Pendolino EMU will work it forward to London Euston unaided, under electric power. Shortly after this picture was taken, the Virgin Trains North Wales services were changed over to Voyager DMUs, removing the need for diesel haulage and ending almost 200 years of locomotive-hauled London Euston to Holyhead services.

37426 and 37521 wait time at Holyhead on 5 March 2000 on 1G79, the 18:27 to Birmingham International. The no-heat 37 tucked inside meant that the train was very cold throughout.

The Class 87s gained a big fan base in their last few years in service, with many followers amassing huge mileages behind their favourite machines. 87006 is seen passing Berkswell in 2004 shoving a Birmingham–London Euston train. 87006 was repainted in an experimental version of the BR Large Logo livery and was later exported to Bulgaria.

On 1 December 2002, RfD-liveried Class 86/2 86210, on hire to Virgin Trains West Coast, pauses at Birmingham International on a London Euston to Birmingham New Street service. A number of Class 86s were hired in around this period, including Class 86/4s, due to the low availability of Virgin's own Class 86s, 87s and 90s.

50031 nears Llanelli on the Fishguard–Cardiff Central Arriva Trains Wales-hauled service on 11 August 2006. ATW hired in 50031 and 50049 from the Class 50 Alliance for the summer dated services.

On 19 May 2006, Fragonset Class 33s 'Bagpipe' 33103 and 'Slim Jim' 33202 pass Berkswell at speed on an empty coaching stock working. Fragonset Railways was formed in 1997 as a spot hire company and bought a number of older locomotives from established operators, including these Class 33s from EWS.

Class 87s were the mainstay for Virgin Trains express West Coast passenger services before the introduction of Pendolino EMUs and their withdrawal from regular service in 2006. Here, 87004 arrives at Coventry on a London Euston–Birmingham New Street service on 24 May 2005.

90027 stands at Birmingham International after rescuing 90014 on 3 June 2009 on a London Euston–Birmingham New Street service.

On 12 May 2009, EWS Class 90 90035 arrives at Birmingham New Street on a service from London Euston, hauling a hired-in rake of Mark 3 coaches. The distinctive Bullring can be seen in the background.

Taken with a long lens, in summer 2000, 37415 passes the remains of Conwy Castle and approaches Llandudno Junction on a Bangor–Crewe service, with a standard rake of Mark 2 pressure-ventilated stock. This stock is popular with enthusiasts as the 'quarter light' windows can be fully opened, allowing the sound of the 37s to be heard inside the train.

The return of long-withdrawn diesel loco classes like Deltics and Westerns to main-line railtour duty in February 2002 proved highly popular with old fans of the locos and younger enthusiasts alike. On Saturday 3 May 2008, Western D1015 *Western Champion* stands at Carlisle on a return railtour to Tame Bridge Parkway. This tour, earlier travelling to and from Edinburgh via the East and West Coast main lines, was the first visit of a Western to Scotland.

On Sunday 4 December 2005, a gala day was organised on the Rhymney Line to commemorate the end of loco-hauled services on the route; there was an hourly timetable in place and representatives of all the classes of the locos that had worked on the branch. 33207 waits the road at Caerphilly on the 11:15 Rhymney–Cardiff Central.

Locomotive haulage doesn't get rarer than this – the only recorded working, other than a railtour or a failure, of a Class 59/2 on a timetabled passenger service. 59206 was fixed to work 1S59, the 12:06 London Paddington–Glasgow on 14 May 2000. This sub-class of 59, recently reallocated from the West Yorkshire coalfields, had a top speed of 75mph and the driver tried to take it up to 100mph between Coventry and Birmingham International. The author confirmed that the speedo was wrong and only 93mph had been achieved, still, it was probably an all-time speed record for a Class 59.

On 27 October 2000, 37601 stands at Coventry on 1V99, the 19:15 Manchester Piccadilly to London Paddington, with 47853 tucked inside. The EPS Class 37s were fairly regular performers on CrossCountry services around this time.

First Great Western began to suffer a DMU shortage at the end of the noughties and, to the delight of local enthusiasts, contracted two Class 67s and a rake of Mark 2 coaches to provide a loco-hauled diagram between Cardiff and Taunton from 11 to 15 December 2009. This short-term solution eventually lasted two years. Here, 67020 waits at Bristol Temple Meads on 7 September 2010 with a service to Taunton.

87001 reacquired the name *Stephenson* from sister loco 87101 in 2003 and was repainted into BR Corporate Blue livery while still in service with Virgin Trains West Coast. Here, later in 2003, the loco arrives at Nuneaton on a diverted service from London Euston to Wolverhampton. 87001 is preserved as part of the National Collection.

The Association of Community Rail Partnerships (ACoRP) held its first ever event over the weekend of Friday 23 to Sunday 25 September at Norwich. In addition to a display of exotic locos in the yard at Norwich, a number of guest locos were provided for additional passenger services. 20096 and 20905 are seen at Lowestoft on an additional to Norwich on Sunday 25 September 2005.

37408 arrives at Birmingham International with an early morning service from Holyhead. At this stage, 37408 was in its well-remembered and popular Large Logo BR Blue livery. The Class 37 would then run around its train and wait for its due departure time back to Holyhead. Terminating trains at International, rather than New Street, prevented station blockages during the run round of locos.

On 23 August 2000, Class 37/7 heavyweight 37895 stands at Llandudno Junction on a Crewe–Holyhead service. The Summer of 2000 proved very popular with fans of no-heat freight Class 37s on North Wales Coast passenger services and 37895 was a particularly rare working.

Class 37/7 heavyweight 37895 approaches Rhyl on 23 August 2000 on a Crewe–Holyhead service. The front coach on this service, and on many other Class 37-hauled trains down the North Wales Coast, was mostly occupied by rail enthusiasts around this time.

On 26 January 2000, 37426 stands at Bangor on a Holyhead to Birmingham New Street working. The front coach was one of the last BR Mark 1s in service on timetabled passenger trains in the UK and was highly popular with bashers and other passengers alike.

On 1 January 2002, ever reliable and well-travelled Class 37 37408 stands at Leeds station after arriving on 1E23, the 13:33 from Carlisle. Arriva North East hired Class 37/4s and stock from EWS to operate these services in 2002 and 2003, with some trains running through. They also worked from Harrogate and York, providing a loco-hauled service over the Settle and Carlisle Railway that was very popular with photographers.

On 13 February 2005, Class 57/3 57312 *The Hood* waits at Preston on 'drag' duty. The new Dellner coupler for haulage of Pendolino EMUs is not needed in this instance, the dragged train being formed of a Class 87 and Mark 3 stock.

86227 *Golden Jubilee* stands at Norwich on the 14:30 to London Liverpool Street on 6 September 2002. The Class 86 had been adorned with a Union Jack as part of the jubilee celebrations for HM The Queen.

Near the end of locomotive-hauled services on Virgin Trains (around the time the Class 390 Pendolino EMUs were being introduced) low availability of the private operator's own fleet of Class 87s and 90s saw them turn regularly to EWS to hire the freight company's locos. In this case, 90039 has been turned out for a London Euston–Birmingham New Street service on 10 August 2007.

Chapter 4

The 2010s

In the 2010s, locomotive haulage saw a little bit of an upturn, after a long period of decline. Locos and stock even returned to the West Coast Main Line on daytime trains, albeit in a limited manner, and for only a short time period. With their Pendolino fleet struggling to achieve the high availability figures needed to work a full West Coast service, Virgin Trains returned a rake of Mark 3 coaches into service in 2009, rebranded into their own livery and booked for haulage behind hired-in Class 90s. In earlier years, the set was used fairly intensively on the Euston–Birmingham–Wolverhampton corridor. In later years, the 19:03 Euston–Birmingham and 20:50 return was a favourite diagram for the set, officially classified as WB64. Also, for a few years the only diagram was the Fridays-only 18:43 London Euston to Crewe via Birmingham. The Class 90s, initially from EWS/DB were later provided by Freightliner then, finally, DRS.

The last working of the Pretendolino set was on 24 October 2014, after which it was transferred to Norwich Crown Point as a spare rake for the Norwich–London Liverpool Street services.

More attractive to haulage enthusiasts was the unprecedented use of Class 37s, and later Class 68s, on Northern's Cumbrian Coast trains from 2015, with some services running through to Preston. Initially, before the introduction of Class 37/4s and DBSOs on these trains later in 2015, the Class 37s were operated in top and tail fashion with a variety of 'no-heat' locos, to the delight of enthusiasts. From 12 March 2018, one of the hauled sets began to be worked by Top and Tail Class 68s (with the trailing Class 68 not providing traction power), with the other set remaining Class 37 powered with a DBSO. The final workings on the Cumbrian Coast with 37s and stock were at the end of December 2018.

The replacement of Class 67s with Class 68s on Chiltern services proved popular with enthusiasts, the new locos being pleasingly noisy with a very quick turn of pace, giving them a new loyal following.

The hire of Class 67s 67006 and 67028 on a series of Rugby additionals from Coventry to Nuneaton in February 2016 was a bold experiment that saw locomotive haulage on the Coventry–Nuneaton branch, unheard of in the diesel era, save for diversions and DMU rescues.

Another line that saw a very unexpected return to locomotive haulage was the Oxenholme–Windermere branch in 2018, due to a shortage of DMUs in June and July 2018. Locomotives and stock were provided by West Coast Railways and saw a Class 37, Class 47, Class 57 and even a Class 33 return to Windermere on stock, a form of travel not available on the line since the early 1970s.

The introduction of Class 68s on Liverpool–Scarborough services in 2019 has been a welcome return to locomotives on the TransPennine route and should see a big uptake in bashers starting or rejoining the hobby. Without a crystal ball, it is hard to predict what will happen over the next ten years, though with locomotive haulage seeing a slight rise in popularity with operators, here's hoping for more pleasant surprises.

Class 52 Western D1015 *Western Champion* leads Class 40 40145 through Tile Hill (between Coventry and Birmingham International) on the *East Lancs Champion* railtour from Crewe to Penzance on Saturday 15 May 2010. Westerns and Class 40s would very rarely have worked in tandem, in service.

On Saturday 20 March 2010, Class 20s 20304 and 20301 pause awaiting time at Birmingham New Street on a 'Spin and Win' (multi-loco) railtour heading for Carlisle.

D5185 (later renumbered as 25035 by BR under the TOPS System) drifts into Quorn on a diesel gala working in 2015, with 26038 on the rear. This working is one of the traditional gala trains from Loughborough to Rothley Brook and return, with top and tail working to avoid the need to run a locomotive round, which enabled additional trains to be pathed into the schedule.

D5830 (later numbered 31297, then 31463, then 31563) is a preserved Class 31, withdrawn in June 1996 and now based on the Great Central Railway at Loughborough. The experimental BR Golden Ochre livery was originally applied to sister loco D5579 in service and, while non-authentic on this loco, it has proved popular with visitors to the heritage line.

24081 (5081) was the last remaining example of a Class 24 in service with BR. It was withdrawn in January 1981 and is now preserved at the Gloucestershire and Warwickshire Railway. Here, it is seen at its new home, departing Winchcombe with a train from Toddington to Cheltenham Racecourse in July 2013. The loco is currently undergoing a major overhaul and it is hoped it will return to service in the not too distant future.

Approaching Wansford from Peterborough, a pair of Class 31s comprising 31271 and 31162 are on the Nene Valley Railway during a diesel gala weekend in October 2012.

Wrexham and Shropshire proved highly popular with enthusiasts and other members of the travelling public alike, providing good value and reliable and comfortable alternative options to Virgin Trains. A small dedicated fleet of Class 67s (67010 and 67012–015) were used on the push-pull Wrexham to London Marylebone trains, calling at some intermediate stations as far as Tame Bridge Parkway. Unable to call at lucrative stations in the West Midlands, due to objections by Virgin, the company was eventually wound up, with the locos and stock passing on to Chiltern.

In the early days of Wrexham and Shropshire services, before the introduction of dedicated refurbished Mark 3 coaches and DVTs, the company hired in stock from Cargo D and Class 67s from the general EWS/DB Schenker pool. In January 2010, 67018 had been repainted in DB Schenker cherry red livery with maple leaf branding and named *Keith Heller*. Here, it is seen just after Canley, west of Coventry, on the rear of a Marylebone service in 2010.

Class 57/3s were gainfully employed by Virgin Trains on many Sundays. Initially, they dragged Classes 86-90 on hauled stock, and later Class 390 EMUs, over the unelectrified section between Birmingham New Street and Nuneaton. Here, 57306 is seen on a diverted London Euston to Wolverhampton service, passing Whitacre Junction. In November 2011, six of the Class 57/3s were transferred to Network Rail as there was little need for them on dragging duties such as this.

The industrial railway serving the Scunthorpe Steel Works is the largest in Europe and includes around 110 miles of track. The Appleby Frodingham Railway Preservation Society is based within the complex and used to organise extensive open days using a variety of on-site and visiting motive power. Until recently, the works used two Class 20s, 20056 and 20066, to haul trains of continuously welded rail around the complex. Here, 20066 is seen operating top and tail with Class 02 D2853 and hauling two Class 108 DMU cars as passenger accommodation, during an open weekend. The author was in the cab by special permission and had the train stop here at this location for a photo, which was taken from a slag heap.

During its September 2012 visit to the Great Central Railway to star in the diesel gala, Class 26 26007 is seen here at the classic photo location of Kinchley Lane, between Quorn and Rothley. Prospective photographers are advised that the location is a long walk from either station and for motorists, access is via a rough, unmade single-track road.

On Saturday 11 and Sunday 12 September 2010, the Great Central Railway hired in Class 26 26007 for its bi-annual diesel gala. 26007 is seen here at Leicester North on a service from Loughborough. This loco, built in 1958 and originally numbered D5000, was the first of the type and is now preserved and based at Barrow Hill.

Class 10 Shunter D4067 *Margaret Ethel – Thomas Alfred Naylor* (numbered 10119 originally) is seen at Loughborough, Great Central Railway, in 2013, during a diesel gala weekend. The Class 10s were of a similar design to the Class 08, the difference being that they had a Blackstone diesel power unit rather than an English Electric one.

On 11 September 2011, Spitfire Railtours hired Deltic 55022 to haul *The Norseman* from King's Cross to Newcastle. The Deltic was in high demand for railtour duties and proved to be a crowd puller for railtour operators. Here, the loco is seen under the iconic roof at York as it pauses to let some passengers escape.

The Class 44, 45 and 46 'Peaks' have a very fanatical following, often referred to as the 'Peak Army', and they still follow their chosen classes albeit, since the 1980s, only on preserved railways with the occasional main line foray with a preserved example. Here, 45115 pauses at Ramsbottom on a Bury–Rawtenstall service on the East Lancashire Railway in 2011.

East Coast-liveried HST 43312 pulls into Newark on 15 January 2012 on an Edinburgh–London King's Cross service. East Coast was one of several operators on the East Coast Main Line franchise that have been in charge of services on the route since privatisation and operated the route directly as a state-owned company from 2009 to 2015.

On 15 August 2017, 37419, with 37405 on the rear, approaches Oulton Broad on a Lowestoft to Norwich service. Greater Anglia had hired Class 37s, Class 68s and two rakes of stock (the 'short sets') to operate services over the 'Wherry Lines' from Norwich to Great Yarmouth and Lowestoft, freeing up DMUs for other services. These loco-hauled trains ended in 2019 with the introduction of new units from Stadler.

68019 waits at Norwich on the rear of a Great Yarmouth service using a 'short set' on 23 March 2017. 68003 was the leading loco. On these services only the leading Class 68 powered, with the loco on the Norwich end of the stock providing electrical train heating. On the 68-hauled services, acceleration was very impressive indeed.

Save for the famous Cliffe-Uddingston cement workings in the 1960s and 1970s, Class 33s have never been common at York, and even rarer on passenger services. The sale of a number of Class 33s to West Coast Railways in 2005 changed that, with the type being seen occasionally on railtour and stock movement duties nationwide. Here, 33207 *Jim Martin* stands at York on a railtour to Whitby on 10 July 2010. Class 37 37678 on the rear prevented the need for run rounds at Battersby.

On 1 August 2013, 67010 passes King's Sutton on a London Marylebone–Birmingham service. Formerly used by Wrexham and Shropshire, the loco and coaches were transferred over to Chiltern Railways with small bodyside branding on the Mark 3 stock and no branding on the Class 67s, which were due to be replaced by brand-new Class 68s, ordered by, and to be leased from, Direct Rail Services.

20189 draws into Amersham with a 4TC set and London Underground ex-Metropolitan Railways electric locomotive *Sarah Siddons* on the rear, on 9 September 2012, as part of the Amersham Heritage Day event organised by LUL. *Sarah Siddons* and a variety of Class 20s were used on these regular services, and at Steam on the Met events, with the Class 20s being provided by the Class 20 Locomotive Society and *Michael Owen* and *Sarah Siddons* coming from the London Transport Museum collection.

The Cumbrian Coast village of St. Bees is an unlikely venue for a locomotive-hauled service but here on 12 September 2018, Class 68033, with 68005 *Defiant* leading, leaves the small station crossing point with a Barrow-in-Furness to Carlisle service. Bashers regularly leapt off at this point for a loco-hauled service passing in the opposite direction.

On 11 May 2015, Class 68 68008 passes King's Sutton with the 17:10 London Marylebone–Kidderminster service. 68008 *Avenger* is a particular favourite with the Class 68 fans and, together with 68009 *Titan*, is one of two DRS-liveried Class 68s equipped with AAR push-pull facilities, which means it can be hired in to Chiltern Railways for standby duties.

On 28 May 2015, 68004 *Rapid* arrives at Aberdour on the evening 'Full Circle' Edinburgh–Fife working. With the usual locomotives, 68006 and/or 68007, unavailable, DRS provided other locos from the fleet.

On 6 May 2012, Class 57/3 57308 *Tin Tin* prepares to leave Coventry while working 1Z14, the 13:43 to London Euston. With Dellner couplers fitted for rescuing Class 390 Pendolino EMUs, the 57/3s were still called on for dragging conventional hauled stock before their replacement.

On Thursday 21 June 2018, 37669, with 57316 on the rear, provides the unprecedented sight of a Class 37 leaving Windermere, hauling 2Z04, the 11:30 to Oxenholme. The remains of the former Windermere Shed (now part of Booth's supermarket) can be seen to the rear. Complaints from some locals regarding the sound from the Class 37 led to it being replaced by a Class 33 then, eventually, a Class 57.

On Saturday 17 June 2017, 68009 *Titan* propels the 13:55 Birmingham Moor Street to London Marylebone Chiltern Railways service southwards from Birmingham. This photo was taken from the roof of the Bullring car park, which is an excellent location for any railway photographers who don't mind occasionally being accused of being car thieves by overzealous security staff.

On Sunday 28 February 2016, Class 67 67006 stands at Nuneaton after arrival on an additional service from Coventry, which was put on for a rugby match being played at the Ricoh Stadium. 67028 was the locomotive at the Coventry end of the stock. The extra trains relieved pressure on the roads to the stadium but heavy losses by the organisers meant that this experiment was, unfortunately, short-lived.

On 10 March 2015, 67001 propels the 'Pauper's Wag' service empty stock (Arriva Trains Wales branded) from Manchester Piccadilly to Longsight Depot after it arrived from Chester with a DVT leading. The set was due to work back to the North Wales Coast after a short break, ending its diagram at Crewe later in the day.

68016 waits at Norwich, on 13 July 2016, with a Wherry Line short set service from Great Yarmouth. At the other end of the rake of coaches, 68019 waits to take the train back out to Lowestoft. The Wherry Line loco-hauled services proved very popular with enthusiasts and the local Wherry Lines Travellers group.

On 3 January 2018, 68007 crosses the world-famous Forth Rail Bridge with the 'Full Circle' evening commuter service from Edinburgh. It would return to Edinburgh, via Glenrothes with Thornton. These services are due to end in 2020 with the introduction of additional EMUs into Scotland.

A minor fall of snow in December 2010 caused travel chaos in the south of England. On 18 December 2010, an unidentified First Great Western HST power car propels a Bristol Temple Meads–London Paddington service out of Bath Spa – it was the first train for several hours. By 2019, HSTs had been withdrawn from all long-distance Great Western express services.

Until the end of 2019, the preserved Class 87 87002 *Royal Sovereign* was still employed on main-line duties on the Caledonian Sleepers, generally taking empty coaching stock to and from Wembley from London Euston but occasionally working trains through to Scotland. On the morning of 29 July 2015, the Class 87 waits to take empty coaching stock from the Highland Sleeper out to Wembley Yard.

From 5 July 2010, the second diagram on the FGW loco-hauled DMU replacement services became Class 67 hauled. Here, on 7 September 2010, 67028 sits on the rear of the loco-hauled set with a service for Taunton; 67020 is the leading train loco. These trains operated up until 12 November 2010, and with Class 67 haulage proved reliable and successful.

DRS's dual-mode Class 88s have become popular guests for preserved railway diesel galas, and are also in great demand by railtour operators. Here, 88004 is seen with 68016 at Appleby after working 1Z40, the Settle and Carlisle explorer, on Saturday 12 August 2017. The two locos were multied up with the Class 88 working on diesel southwards over the Settle and Carlisle Line until reaching the West Coast overhead wires again, just south of Preston.

The sight of a 60-year-old Class 20 working a timetabled public passenger service was unlikely in the 21st century. However, on Tuesday 9 February 2010, 20304, shown at Norwich with a Great Yarmouth service, deputised for a non-available Class 47/4. Electric train heating was provided by a Class 47 at the far end of the stock. This may have been, other than additionals and rescues, the last ever Class 20 to work a timetabled passenger service.

On 17 October 2019, 91119 waits at Edinburgh Waverley before taking an ECS out to Craigentinny Depot. This loco has been repainted into original InterCity Swallow livery (as applied when new) for its last few years in service on the East Coast route.

On 12 December 2017, DRS-liveried Chiltern standby loco Class 68009 *Titan* waits time at Birmingham Snow Hill with the 16:10 London Marylebone to Kidderminster service.

On 17 January 2019, 90015 pauses at Ipswich on a Liverpool Street–Norwich working. These Great Eastern services are due to be completely replaced by Stadler 'Flirt' units by the end of 2019, ending another long association between a well-known main line and locomotive haulage.

Standing in for an unavailable Chiltern Railways Class 67, 67020 stands at Birmingham Moor Street on 2 February 2015. This was one of the last workings for an EWS Class 67 on Chiltern, and the Class 68s started to take over these services shortly after this photo was taken.

67008 propels a Birmingham Moor Street to London Marylebone service into Leamington Spa on 20 April 2015. Chiltern had taken over the Wrexham and Shropshire Mark 3 stock for these services and continued to hire Class 67s as motive power.

On 17 January 2019, 90013 pauses at Ipswich on a Norwich–Liverpool Street working. The Class 90s are due to be phased out of use on the Greater Anglia Main Line in the near future, to be replaced by new Stadler 'Flirt' units.

On Mazey Day (Saturday 25 June) 2011, DRS Class 20s 20308 and 20309 await departure from Gloucester on a railtour from Birmingham International to Penzance. Class 57 57601 is on the rear to provide electric train heating.

Ex-Metropolitan Railway electric loco Bo-Bo *Sarah Siddons* leaves Harrow on the Hill with the empty stock, bound for Neasden after a number of special workings on Sunday 12 September 2011. 20227 from the Class 20 Locomotive Society is on the rear of the LT-owned 4TC set.

Arriva Trains Wales-liveried Class 57/3 57314 stands at Crewe on the Northbound 'Wag' train from Cardiff Central to Holyhead in 2010.

Unusually, on the southern end of the stock at London Marylebone (due to a number of route diversions and reversals), Class 67 67015 stands at the London Terminus in 2010.

Class 40 40106 features elsewhere in this book, as it has been in service for almost 40 years. The locomotive, now owned by the Class 40 Preservation Society, is still as popular as ever. As its steam-heating boiler is still serviceable, it has been providing motive power for some winter trains on the Severn Valley Railway, as here at Bridgnorth on 23 November 2019, working the 17:10 to Kidderminster.

An LNER HST (powered by power cars 43319 and 43314) waits at Newcastle on the 1-hour-late-running 1W24, the 16:00 London King's Cross–Aberdeen service on 5 December 2019. This was one of the last few weeks of service for HSTs on King's Cross trains and while the HSTs continued to give exemplary performance, late running on the East Coast Main Line had become endemic.

On Saturday 7 September 2019, 68027 waits at Scarborough on 1F62, the 10:41 Scarborough to Liverpool Lime Street TransPennine Express service. The introduction of these 'Nova 3' sets has proved troublesome on TPE as there are many issues with the new Mark 5 coaches and also with training and train crew provision.

On Bank Holiday Monday, 26 August 2019, a series of railtours were operated between London Marylebone, Rickmansworth and Quainton Road, in connection with an open day being held at the latter. Here, BR Blue Class 20 20007 leads London Transport-liveried 20142 *Sir John Betjeman* with the LT 4TC set and Class 33 D6515 (33012) *Lt. Jenny Lewis RM* on the rear on 1Z34, the 12:25 Quainton Road–Rickmansworth.

On Saturday 18 May 2019, 68011 leaves High Wycombe heading for London on 1H37, the 13:55 Birmingham Moor Street–London Marylebone service.

On 9 November 2019, 68026 waits at Liverpool Lime Street on 1J53, the 20:56 to Stalybridge. After arrival there, the set was due to go empty to Longsight.

40106 passes Foley Park, Severn Valley Railway, on 22 June 2019, past the very impressive poppy field in full bloom.

Further reading from

As Europe's leading transport publisher, we produce a wide range of market-leading railway magazines.